Build it! Grow it! Sell it!

Nine Steps to a Thriving Contracting Business

by Lynn Wise

Copyright © 2014 Lynn Wise

All rights reserved.

ISBN-13: 978-1500966911
ISBN-10: 1500966916

CONTENTS

	Introduction	1
1	Communicate Your Goals and Vision	4
2	Business Financial Dashboard	22
3	Reliable Revenue Streams and Market Trends	36
4	Build a Great TEAM!	46
5	Create Training Systems	56
6	The Yellow Pages are Dead	64
7	Automated Systems Improve Your Bottom Line	86
8	Accountability	95
9	Freedom in Your Future	100
	Conclusion	108
	About the Author	110

INTRODUCTION

It's no accident that you've picked up this book. You're either the owner of a contracting business, and you're concerned about the growth and success of your business; or you know someone in the industry, and you're concerned about their success. Either way, you'll find the answers you're looking for in this book.

I share techniques, strategies, and inside information that will ensure the success of your contracting business.

My story with the contracting business began when I was eighteen years old. I had just graduated from high school a semester early and had no plans for my future. It was the dead of winter, and our furnace went out. When the business owner came to fix it, he offered me a job, and I took it.

I'd had no work experience, but now I was a service dispatcher, answering the phone and delegating jobs to the technicians. It sounded simple, but I soon realized this was a big job. I needed far more information from the caller than just a name and address.

I needed to ask questions – the *right* questions. I needed more knowledge to do the job with excellence and to be of value to the business. I told the owner I needed more training.

I began to learn exactly what questions to ask in order for the service team to be efficient and effective. In fact, the owner allowed me to learn all aspects of running the business.

Over the next fifteen years, I led his business to increased sales and company value, and became an equity owner in the company.

I knew I needed formal education to reach the next level in business, so I left that contracting firm and earned my MBA in finance. I then spent nearly twenty years in corporate sales and management. Over the last thirty-five years, I've owned five successful small businesses in retail, distribution, and direct sales.

Owning the contracting firm and retail stores, being a wholesale distributor, my experience in corporate sales, with a Yellow Page company, then with IBM has led me full circle. I am now returning to my true passion: helping small contractor companies build wealth.

My varied experiences have given me a clear understanding of why the company owner at my first job struggled to grow his business with purpose and value. I now understand why he was unable to grow it to be an asset for him and the other investors.

It was pretty simple, actually. First, he thought too small. And second, he didn't know how to empower an effective team that could have helped make the business successful.

With the clear vision I've achieved through my years of experience and education, I now want to help other contractors avoid the same mistakes.

Now that you know my story and my purpose, let's get started.

1

Communicate Your Goals and Vision

I was ready to crawl into bed after a long day when my phone rang. It was a contractor named Marty whom I'd worked with several years earlier. He didn't sound good. In fact, he was calling from his hospital bed following a bad accident in his company truck. The truck had been totaled, and he'd been in intensive care for several days.

Marty's Dilemma

"If I'm hard to understand," he said, "it's because my jaw is wired shut. On top of that, my leg's broken, I have back problems, and it looks like I'll be laid up for a while. I can't work. I've lost my company. I've lost everything." I remembered this contractor as being a man of high integrity. He was good at what he did, and his customers liked him. I think he called me because he just needed someone to talk to. His wife had to take a second job in an effort to save their home. I felt horrible for Marty.

I asked him about insurance. He was fortunate that his health insurance would cover his medical expenses, and his vehicle insurance would pay off the truck. But there was no cash for the mortgage, the utilities, or the groceries.

Marty had three employees: a part-time office helper, a young apprentice, and a trained technician. In the first few days of Marty's hospitalization, no one knew what to do or where to find anything. His wife didn't know enough about the business to be much help.

Marty had to resort to sending calls to a competitor. I asked if he thought he could get his old customers back once he had recovered. "Doubt it," was his reply.

Marty's business evaporated.

He Owned a *Job*

What if this happened to you? Would you be in the same spot? It's not a pretty picture.

Here's the upshot: Marty didn't own a business; he owned a *job*. And a crappy job, at that. He worked long hours, rarely took a vacation, charged too little, had no retirement plan, and operated with a thin cash flow for the business.

What could Marty have done differently? There are several parts to the answer.

Running a Business

Most contractors are great at what they do. They're reliable, trustworthy, fair, and they truly care about their customers. They do a great job in the field. In fact, it's in the field that they shine.

The problem is, most have not invested the same amount of

time, energy, commitment, and education into becoming a smart business owner. It takes just as much skill to run and operate a successful business as it does to repair faucets and unplug toilets.

If you're like most contractors I've known, you started out with your pickup and a few tools, applying your knowledge in the best way you knew how. Because you did a good job and because customers relied on you and told friends and neighbors about you, your business grew. It grew gradually until one day you realized you needed help, more and better equipment, and possibly added financing to get it all done.

So, what's the problem?

Out of Balance

The problem is, the business became out of balance. The practical side of the business was flourishing, while the other side (planning, management, and communication) went begging.
This was Marty's main problem.

Marty never thought about future goals. He had just taken one day at a time and hoped everything would turn out okay in the end.

Where are You?

Where are you in that spectrum? Do you know where you're going? Do you know how to get there?

Let's back up for a minute. You may be saying, "Hey Lynn, what does any of this have to do with communication?"

Glad you asked!

The crux of the matter is this: you cannot communicate what you don't know. You cannot communicate what you have not identified and clarified for yourself. You cannot communicate fuzzy thoughts and ideas. It's time to pay attention to the core elements of what it takes to create an *asset* – not just a go-to-work-everyday job.

Being a good businessperson is no harder than being a good contractor. Both have to do with learning and commitment. Realize that the effects of poor management can be devastating to the performance of a company. Many business owners blame employees for poor service, financial losses, and low-quality products, when the fault lies in poor management, poor planning, and poor communication.

It's easier to muddle through each day than to stop and

reflect. But ask yourself this: *why are you in business*? Why do you get up and go to work every day?

- Do you love your trade?
- Do you love what you're doing?
- Do you enjoy helping people?
- Do you just want to *make a living?*
- Do you want to create a business that will build a good living for you and your family today, and possibly a retirement for you in the future – a business that will actually be a salable asset when you are ready to step out of the picture?

If you've never answered this question, today's the day. More questions will come, but the answer to this one will become your plumb line. You may have to think about it for a few days.

I challenge you to set aside time each day to journey through the tasks and action steps given in this book. Remember, the time you invest in becoming a knowledgeable business owner is going to pay big dividends down the road.

Think for a moment about a football coach who has no clue:

- How to motivate his players.
- How to create winning game plans.
- How to teach and communicate those game plans.
- How to study and learn from the opposing teams.
- How to deal with players' families and other interested parties.

If the coach knows all there is to know about football, does any of this matter? Of course it matters. Every item in the list above matters a great deal when it comes to building a winning team.

You need a game plan for your business. Identify:

- Why are you in business?
- What do you want your business to achieve?
- What are your goals for building the business?
- What are your core values, and how does your business reflect them?
- Who is your target client?
- How will you handle growth in your business?
- How will you create your own business brand?
- How will you study and learn from the competition?

- How will you stand apart from the competition?

The answers to these questions will be the foundation on which you will build.

Create a Business Plan

The most effective way to begin this identification process is with a business plan, and *it's not that hard.* In fact, once you get into it, you'll be surprised at how fascinating planning can be.

How the heck do I write up a business plan? you ask.

1. Check with the SBA (Small Business Administration) at www.sba.gov. You'll find a workable, easy-to-use, business plan template on this site.

2. Get yourself an accountability partner, such as a business coach. We'll talk more about this later in the book, but this is a great resource for your future growth and success.

Not Set in Stone

A business plan is a flexible, ever-growing document. While it may not take you to your final destination, it can definitely get you to next month, next quarter, and next year. You will be amazed at how much clarity comes from creating a business plan. As you begin to give serious thought to why you're in business, what goals you are setting, and how you will achieve them, you'll find that rather than just muddling through, you have a charted course.

The writing out of plans, ideas, and visions for your business, in effect, stirs up your subconscious mind. You've given that quiet part of your mind something to chew on. Now ideas will begin to pop as to exactly how these plans can be executed.

When to Start

Start your business plan today. Jump on it. It doesn't matter if you've been in business for ten years, or ten months. The sooner you get cracking on this, the sooner you'll get your game plan on and start building winning business strategies.

Your answers to the questionnaire at the end of this chapter will be the basis for your business plan.

Planning Precedes Communication

I said earlier that you cannot communicate what is unclear in your own mind. Once you begin to work on your business plan, you can start communicating this vision to yourself and others. Once your plan is in place, and you are communicating the direction and vision of the company, your employees, other team members, and your family will all be on the same page.

Ever watch a football game where the players work together to execute the plays? It's a beautiful thing, right? This can be a model for your company: everyone working together as a team.

How Employees Perceive Value

Many contractors believe that as long as they pay an employee a decent salary and promptly, s/he will be happy. This is not necessarily true. Of course, they want to be paid, but they also want to be valued. What does this mean? An employee feels valued to the degree that s/he is included in the plans and vision for the company. Workers will actually go to a lower-paying job if they feel more valued there.

People love to be a part of a winning situation, part of a bigger vision. How did Bill Gates keep his buddies hanging in with him when no money was coming in? They all knew they were a vital part of something much bigger than themselves: they were launching

Microsoft. If your employees know what you are trying to achieve, you'll have more than their time: you'll have their hearts.

An Added Benefit

An added benefit comes when you begin to communicate your goals and visions: *other people will begin to feed you ideas.* As you share with your spouse, family members, employees, and business associates, they will have tips and strategies that would never have occurred to you.

Business Meetings

If you thought business meetings were only for the white-collar corporate dudes, you're missing an opportunity. Gather your people around you. Seek their ideas and feedback. Listen to them. Create a survey or questionnaire and find out what they perceive, what they think, what they need.

Once you establish weekly business meetings and open up communications, you'll kick yourself for not starting sooner.

Acquiring Financing

Until you've verbalized, or put in writing, your plans, goals, and visions for your company, you'll have trouble getting financing for future growth.

The first thing a lender will ask for is a business plan. Without it, you're dead in the water. Why not get it prepared now, before the need arises?

Target Market

Writing your business plan forces you to zero in on your target market. Whom do you want to do business with? What geographical location?

At first glance, this may seem like a strange concept. To many contractors, the target market is anyone who needs their services.

But that thinking can lead you down a dead end road. Without carefully defining a target market, you'll say yes to anyone. But you won't know *why* you said yes. That's not a good position to be in.

Define your ideal client base:

- What do they look like?
- What are their ages?

- Where do they live?

- What's their income level?

- What kind of cars do they drive?

- How many children do they have?

The fancy word for this is *demographics*, but it translates into more profit and more success in your business.

Here's an example. Kevin has a heat and air business that services a roughly fifty-mile radius. One day he got a call from a potential customer from two counties over. At first glance, this job had the potential to pull in more revenue than any of his current projects. Kevin couldn't resist. He bid that contract and got it. Now his troubles began.

He quickly realized that he didn't know the area. He didn't know the suppliers there or if he could get credit with them. He was unfamiliar with the licensing codes. The distance meant some of his workers were operating out-of-pocket, and he couldn't move them about as easily as when they worked locally. Then there was the cost of gas to travel the distance each day.

Because Kevin had never established his *preferred*

demographics for his business, he had no reason to turn this job down. The bigger job wound up netting very little profit. It became an expensive lesson, but one he wouldn't forget.

Once Kevin set his plan in motion and identified his demographics, his customer service reps knew immediately when to turn down a potential job.

Who Are You? What Do You Do Best?

Lack of planning and lack of communication means you will fail to identify your company's strengths. You will never clearly identify what sets you apart from the competition. What are the problems you solve and what makes your solutions better? Why would a potential customer call you versus others in the business?

Without this knowledge, you won't stand out, and you will be forever relegated to the gray area of being *just another contractor.*

Summary

Communication and the planning that precedes it are the foundations upon which you build. If it is weak and faulty, the whole structure of your business will also be weak and faulty. It's time to make some changes to ensure future success.

In the next chapter, we'll look at your company's finances and how you can get on top of things and *stay in control*.

Chapter 1 Actions Steps

- Stop running in circles. Take time to ask hard questions about you, your business, and your future.
- Determine where you're going and how you're going to get there.
- Whatever it takes – time, commitment, learning curve – create your business plan.
- Create a survey/questionnaire for your employees to get their feedback.
- Schedule regular meetings with your employees to facilitate communication.

Chapter 1 Addendum: Business Plan Questionnaire

The answers to these questions will be the framework for your business plan.

EXECUTIVE SUMMARY

- Why will the business succeed?
- What do you want to start (or change)?
- How much money is required?
- What is the return on the investment?
- Why is the venture a good risk?

BUSINESS DESCRIPTION

- What type of business are you planning?
- What products or services will you sell?
- What type of opportunity is it (new, part time, expansion, seasonal, year round)?
- Why does it promise to succeed?
- What is the growth potential?
- How is it unique?

MARKETING

- Who are your potential customers?
- How large is the market?
- Who are your competitors? How are their businesses positioned?
- What market share do you anticipate?
- How will you price your product or service?

- What advertising and promotional strategies will you use?

ORGANIZATION

- Who will manage the business?
- What qualifications do you have?
- How many employees will you need? What will they do?
- How will you structure your organization?
- What are your plans for employee salaries, wages, and benefits?
- What consultants and specialists will you need? How will you use them?
- What legal form of ownership will you choose? Why?
- What licenses and permits will you need?

CRITICAL RISKS

- What potential problems could arise?
- How likely are they?
- How do you plan to manage these potential problems?

FINANCIAL

- What is your total estimated business income for the first year? Monthly for the first year? Quarterly for the second and third years?
- What will it cost you to open the business?
- What will your personal monthly financial needs be?
- What sales volume will you need in order to make a profit the first three years?
- What will be the break-even point?

- What will be your projected assets, liabilities, and net worth on the day before you expect to open?
- What are your total financial needs?
- What are your potential funding sources? How will you spend it?
- How will the loans be secure?

MILESTONE SCHEDULE

- What timing have you projected for this project?
- How have you set your objectives?
- Have you set up your deadlines for each stage of your venture?
- Is there a relationship between events in this venture?

APPENDIX

- Have you included all important documents, drawings, agreements, and references?

2

Business Financial Dashboard

On the dashboard of your truck is an instrument panel with lighted dials and gauges, and sometimes flashing warning lights. These are *indicators* that give you information about what is going on under the hood. If the vehicle overheats, you'll see that dial swinging to the "H" position. If the oil light comes on, you need to check out what's wrong. These indicators are there for a reason; ignore them at your peril.

Key Performance Indicators

Your business also has a number of indicators called **Key Performance Indicators** (**KPIs**). As with your truck's instrument panel, you need to learn about these indicators and then monitor them in your business operations to measure and assess performance.

Four Key Areas to Monitor with KPIs

Most contractors work with a CPA and a bookkeeper to keep up with monthly financial statements, the profit and loss statement, and the balance sheet. You need these reports to monitor the numbers and the tax implications of your business operations. Most service contractors miss this important step: to *understand what these reports are telling you*. There's more here than just the bottom line.

You need to know what the **KPIs** are telling you and why you should care. For instance, if you had to liquidate to get cash in hand tomorrow, how quickly could you do it? Monitoring your **KPIs** can give you early warning signals of problems and changes in your business.

Liquidity: Cash Flow and Your Access to Cash

Any valuable business needs sufficient cash flows to pay the overhead, employee wages, and expenses. The goals are to keep the cash flow ahead of the debts and operating expenses, and to have a cushion in the bank. One of the key areas to monitor is your ability to pay your short-term debt obligations, such as equipment loans, truck loans, and accounts payable for inventories. You generate working capital to pay these obligations with accounts receivables and cash. When small businesses *go out of business* or *bankrupt,* it's not because they do not make a profit, but because they *run out of cash*.

A great ratio to use is the **current ratio,** which indicates a company's ability to meet short-term obligations. This is calculated by **dividing current assets by current liabilities.** The target value should be at least **2.0**. In other words, your business needs to have at least twice as many current assets as current liabilities.

In addition to the **current ratio**, a business can look at the **quick ratio**. The **quick ratio** is known as the "acid test" and is a quick indication of a company's health. The ratio calculation highlights the cash or liquid assets of your business. The calculation is **(current assets minus inventory) divided by current liabilities**.

You may think that inventory is a liquid asset. It is liquid but some of it is slow moving or sold for below costs. So, to get a good picture of the "cash health" of your business, you **subtract inventory from current assets** to determine how well you can pay your current liabilities.

Current liabilities include short-term debts and accounts payables. The target **quick ratio** is **1.0**, which demonstrates that the liquid assets (e.g., cash and accounts receivables) can pay for current liabilities.

The **liquidity ratios** are a window into the working capital health of your business. A bank or an investor looks to see if the business capital is "working" or paying for fixed assets such as buildings, fancy office equipment, or shop equipment.

Efficiency Ratios: How Well Are You Using the Assets in Your Business?

In business, you need to know if the investments in your assets are delivering a return as part of your business portfolio. Do you know how well you utilize your investments in trucks, equipment, buildings, and current assets to drive sales and profits in your business?

A **KPI** to monitor asset utilization is the **Return on Assets (ROA)**. It calculates a ratio of the **total sales divided by the total assets** of your company. **ROA** tells you how well your assets are being used to generate sales. The target for this ratio should be no less than **2.0**. Less than 2.0 is an indicator that assets are underutilized to drive sales and profits in your company. It might be time to sell some trucks, a building, or at least not buy fancy office equipment. The **ROA** might be telling you it's time to have a "business garage sale."

We can't leave this section without discussing the **Days Sales Outstanding (DSO) KPI**. Most contractors give their customers thirty days to pay off their accounts. I recommend a policy of only extending credit to high volume customers with good credit. Contractors and businesses commonly accept full payment or down payments from credit cards.

The ratio takes into account an average 30.4 days per month to help you determine the time it takes your company to collect outstanding accounts receivables. The average **DSO** is acceptable between 30 and 45 days. Anything past 45 days is viewed risky and impacts your business cash flow. The average **DSO** calculation is **(total accounts receivable times average days in a month) divided by total monthly sales.**

Leverage Ratios: Impact of Debt on Your Business

Understanding your financial status will help you grow your business. Most businesses look for capital so they can grow, but this can be risky if not managed properly.

You can finance growth from owner equity, bank loans, and other investors. The latter involves contractual agreements with interest obligations. Contractual agreements can be risky, though, should your business go through an economic dip or any catastrophic situation, such as a personal injury or a lawsuit.

New customers are knocking on your door. Do you keep saying, "No"? Or do you take orders? If you choose to grow, you must know how to fund that growth. Some will happen internally in the business. But chances are, sooner or later, you'll need investment capital, whether that comes from your own money, angel investors, or the bank.

Some owners are blind-sided by growth. It may be a good growth strategy to expand to a new territory, or add a new employee, or purchase new equipment. You must monitor your **debt ratios**, even if growth is not immediate. I recommend you look at the **debt to total asset ratio (total debt divided by total assets)**. A ratio of **.50 to 1.00** is usually acceptable if you need to get financing. However the closer the ratio is to 1.0, the higher the interest rate from financial lenders. Essentially, the higher the ratio, the riskier your business looks to the outside world.

An additional helpful ratio and risk indicator is the **debt to equity ratio**. The calculation is **total liabilities divided by total equity.** This **KPI** indicates how much is *owned* verses how much is *owed*. The target of this ratio is **1.0** or less. A ratio that is greater than 1.0 indicates that the assets of the company are financed with debt rather than equity. It also points to more risk if you should need to acquire financing for equipment, expansion, etc.

Profitability Ratios: Are you Making Money?

Is your business making money (profit)? Remember, increasing sales does not equal profit. Contractors operate on thin profit margins, and one unforeseen job issue can mean you are working for NO PROFIT!

As a business owner, you need to at least make a return on the financial investment in your company that is equal to any other financial vehicle in the marketplace. Profits are essential for funding growth and to build cash assets to protect the company from economic and market downturns.

Let's start with the **Return on Sales (ROS) ratio**, which provides insight into how profitable company sales are. It is the **net profit divided by gross sales**. The service contractor's ROS average is 2 percent, according to the First Research.

The **Return on Investment (ROI) ratio** shows how much the owner is making on investments in a business. The owner should compare this ratio to other market investments, such as mutual funds, stocks, bonds, etc., to see if the investments are better left in the company or put into other market investments. This ratio is the **net profit of a current period divided by the net worth at the beginning of a year**. The goal of monitoring this ratio is to make sure the current return is comparable to or better than any other investment. This tells the owner whether the business investment is eroding or increasing in returns.

In addition to having the bookkeeper give you a **Profit and Loss (P&L)** statement and a balance sheet, you need a monthly **KPI Dashboard report**. It's the key ratios of your financial statements that provide historical and current insight into your business health. As the company owner, you need to become familiar with the performance-to-drive cash flow, pay debt, finance capital investments, and management of assets and profitability.

Making a Profit on Products and Services

You're not in business to give products and services away. Clearly, you must make a profit.

Knowing your gross profit percent, you can adjust your selling prices to improve. Gross profit dollars must be greater than overhead expenses or you'll be in the proverbial black hole of red ink.

Be sure you calculate selling prices correctly. I find some contractors still multiply their costs by 1.40, thinking they're getting a 40 percent margin. For that margin, the correct calculation is to divide costs by .60 to determine the mark up. For example if your job costs are $100, you divide by .60 which results in 1.66. Your mark-up is $100 costs multiplied by 1.66. This gives you a selling price of $166. If you had multiplied by 1.40, your selling price would be $140, which leaves $26 on the table. If you made that mistake on several hundred work orders, you'd have a no-profit and no-cash business. Profit is a condition of management, not sales.

Sales Target KPIs

Business owners traditionally require a lot of their technicians, and those technicians deserve to know what's expected of them. (This goes back to the importance of communication we discussed in Chapter 1.)

Achieving sales goals in many companies is like playing darts blindfolded. How can the technician hit a goal s/he can't see?! You need to communicate the sales targets and goals for your technicians and salespeople.

When you break down the annual sales using historical trends, the sales figures become more accurate. For example, break down the annual truck goal to weekly sales figures.

When I coach contracting companies, I use the following numbers for goals:

- $160,000 for companies doing less than $2 million (in annual sales)
- $180,000 for companies doing less than $3 million
- $200,000+ for companies exceeding $3 million

Let's use the first example of $160,000. This figure requires a technician to average $3,100 per week, or $615 per day. If your technicians run about three service calls per day, the average invoice must be at least $205.

As you communicate your goals to your technicians, present these numbers. The numbers are in black and white, indisputable and measurable. Technicians know where they stand, and they know what to expect. No more guesswork.

Summary

Step by step, you can take control of the financial aspect of your business. As you grow in this area, collaborate with your bookkeeper and CPA to keep your business on target. They will hold you accountable and keep you on track to assess and implement strategies and systems to achieve the targets.

Chapter 2 Action Steps

- Incorporate a **KPI** dashboard into the monthly financial review of your business.
- Review and implement a mark-up on products and services that will deliver the profits for your business.
- Incorporate your **KPIs** into your business plan, and collaborate with your bookkeeper/accountant to keep your business on track to maintain healthy targets in key areas.
- Set sales targets and goals for your technicians and salespeople.

Chapter 2 Addendum: Guide to Key Performance Indicators (KPIs)

Liquidity Ratios

The liquidity ratios are financial Key Performance metrics that are used to determine a company's ability to pay off its short-terms debts obligations. Generally, the higher the value of the ratio, the more likely a company can cover the short-term debts.

$$\textbf{Current Ratio} = \frac{\text{Current Assets}}{\text{Current Liabilites}} = \frac{\$500,000}{\$250,000} = \textbf{2.0}$$

$$\textbf{Quick Ratio} = \frac{\text{Current Assets} - \text{Inventory}}{\text{Current Liabilites}} = \frac{\$500,000 - \$100,000}{\$250,000} = \textbf{1.6}$$

Efficiency Ratios

Efficiency ratios are typically used to analyze how well a company uses its assets and liabilities internally. Efficiency Ratios can calculate the turnover of receivables, the repayment of liabilities, the quantity and usage of equity and the general use of inventory and machinery.

$$\textbf{Return on Assets} = \frac{\text{Total Sales}}{\text{Total Assets}} = \frac{\$1,500,000}{\$750,000} = \textbf{2.0}$$

Avg Age of Accts Receivables

$$= \frac{\text{Total AR} \times (30.4 \text{ Days})}{\text{Total Monthly Sales}} = \frac{\$130,000 \times 30.4 \text{ Days}}{\$100,000} = \textbf{39.52 Days}$$

Leverage Ratios

A leverage ratio is any ratio used to calculate the financial leverage of a company to get an idea of the company's methods of financing or to measure its ability to meet financial obligations. There are several different ratios, but the main factors looked at include debt, equity, assets and interest expenses.

$$\textbf{Debt to Asset} = \frac{\text{Total Debt}}{\text{Total Assets}} = \frac{\$400{,}000}{\$750{,}000} = .53$$

$$\textbf{Debt to Equity} = \frac{\text{Total Liabilities}}{\text{Total Equity}} = \frac{\$650{,}000}{\$1{,}500{,}000} = .43$$

Profitability Ratios

Profitability ratios are used to assess a business's ability to generate earnings as compared to its expenses and other relevant costs incurred during a specific period of time. For most of these ratios, they are compared to industry averages or competitors. Also, a comparison can be made to the stock market or other financial market investments.

$$\textbf{Return on Sales} = \frac{\text{Net Profit}}{\text{Net Worth}} = \frac{\$25{,}000}{\$180{,}000} = 13.8\%$$

$$\textbf{Return on Investment} = \frac{\text{Net Profit}}{\text{Net Worth}} = \frac{\$25{,}000}{\$180{,}000} = 13.8\%$$

3

Reliable Revenue Streams & Market Trends

One of the biggest factors that will increase your company's value is the extent to which you can predict where future sales will come from. If your business starts from scratch each month, your company's value will be lower than if you can demonstrate the source(s) of your future revenue.

A recurring revenue stream acts like a powerful pair of binoculars for you (and a potential acquirer) to see months or years into the future. Creating an annuity stream is the best way to increase the desirability and value of your company. The surer your future revenue is, the higher the market value of your business.

In the contracting business, one key recurring revenue stream is the service agreements on products and services that you offer new and existing clients. I won't discuss selling the agreements in this chapter, but will cover the benefits for your bottom line and value of your company.

Service agreements are a win–win for your customers and your company. They act as a safety net for most homeowners for the repair and replacement of expensive and necessary appliances and systems in their homes. For your company, they offer a reliable and predictable revenue stream.

Most contracting businesses are running at about 40 percent full-time productivity of their service technicians. That translates into 60 percent underutilization of trucks, equipment, and technician time. The percentages vary among companies and types of services, but in general, the gap is wide and deep. Your goal is to be profitable to build for growth and cash flow needs. Service agreements are a key tool to drive this for contractors.

Contractors have resisted offering service agreements because they feel like they can't make a profit on these agreements. The goal is to make a profit and increase cash flows. To be profitable on service agreements is not a factor of pricing, but a factor of you knowing the most profitable services your technicians deliver and sell. Once your know the profitable services, you can increase the likelihood that your service agreement revenue streams are profitable.

Pick the Winners

Contracting companies are notorious for grouping repair, replacement, and remodel skills into one skill set. You expect a technician to do all of the repairs and replacement work. This approach results partly from not hiring highly skilled technicians and partly from not training your techs in the skills and processes involved in typical repairs. This is a matter of analyzing typical repairs, thus making the skills and processes trainable, repeatable and valuable.

In my experience, service technicians perform differently in different areas. For example, heating technicians may varying skills in dealing with gas, oil, and hot water heating. Although each product is unique for diagnosis and repair, contractors often consider heating repair techs as equal, when they are not.

Start by reviewing the work orders and callbacks in service areas, and analyze where your business is most profitable. When a given technician performs similar repairs repeatedly, s/he becomes very efficient. Training and categorizing your work orders with the appropriately trained technicians makes a reliable and efficient process. Document the training in writing and on videotape, if possible, so you can use it to train new hires or existing technicians in your profitable process.

Analyze the Situation

An analysis begins with pulling your work orders from the last six to twelve months. The first step is to categorize your services into product, repair, and replacement areas. The following is an example for analyzing the work orders of an HVAC contractor:

- Brand of equipment (Bryant, Trane, etc.)

- Type of system (warm air, hot water or electric)
- Type of fuel (gas, oil, electricity)
- Service call type (no heat, no cool, fan runs, fan won't start, etc.)
- Repair results (thermostat replacement, valve replacement, fan motor replacement, etc.)
- Work order sales amount
- Breakdown of work order (profit, labor, material, taxes)
- Service technician assigned to work order

This type of categorization of your work orders gives you a structure to review. This review will give you the insight to determine the most profitable type of service, brand, and technician assignments. At this point, you can build a teachable, repeatable, and valuable process for your key profit areas. I recommend getting the technicians involved in organizing the training program for your company. It gives them a sense of pride and accomplishment, and they will be your advocates for the programs.

Once the review is complete, you can bundle the most common and profitable services in a service agreement. The pricing of the service agreement is another topic, but it should offer the customer a biannual safety maintenance check on several key areas in the home at a discount over an unscheduled service call.

Benefits

Service agreements are a tool to establish predictable and recurring revenues for your company. The benefits include:

- Opportunities to review customers' systems and prevent emergencies because of regular contact (once or twice a year).
- Establishing loyalty with your target customers.
- Establishing and documenting training programs for profitable services.
- Including and rewarding technicians in training programs, which gives them a sense of ownership.
- Creating predictable and repeatable revenue streams for your business.

Creating Differentiation

It seems to be a tradition for contracting companies to offer the same types of services and differentiate on price, skills, and legacy of their company. However, the highly successful contractors dig deeper and innovate their companies and brand by offering unique approaches or products to set themselves apart from their competitors.

A great example of one HVAC contractor approach is to offer repair and installations of outside kitchen grilles and fireplace inserts. The technician skills are similar to the HVAC skills. It's easy to imagine how you could train a technician to specialize in this area. A similar approach would be to do hot tub repairs and replacements in the plumbing product area. The point here is to find a way to offer products and services that set you above the competition.

SMART Home

The SMART home movement is here. One could interpret this to only those appliances or components that can be controlled by a smart phone application, but could extend to any appliance, equipment, or fixture that operates with touch or has an electronic control.

The younger generation customers, such as the Millennial

and Generation Y demographics, are target markets for these services and products. It is great time to educate and offer products and services with the new technological features. Consider hiring and training technicians to show customers how to use smart phone applications. You could also get with the manufacturers and create a teachable, repeatable, and valuable training process and product offering in this space.

Embracing new products positions your company as a forward-thinking innovator. These products should be bundled with service agreements as part of the sales process.

Summary

Recurring revenues are critical to establish predictable revenues for your company. They are also a key factor in increasing the market value of your business and the probability of securing better offers from potential buyers.

Service contractors can offer service agreements on products and services they sell to their customers. Service agreements also create touch points with your customer base to build loyalty and to gain referrals for new customers. Training of repeatable services for the field and increased profit margins are key benefits of service agreements, as well.

Product trends such as SMART Home offer new revenue streams for your business. Offering differentiated or related products can set a company apart from its competitors. This also allows a business to build a unique component into its brand in a market or industry.

Chapter 3 Action Steps

- Establish a regular work order review to determine your company's most profitable types of services and products.
- Develop a service agreement product that will sell maintenance reviews and services to new and existing customers.
- Develop a plan to differentiate your company with products and services, setting your company apart from the competition.

- Embrace technology and innovation in the products and services you sell, and become an expert in these new areas to differentiate your brand in your marketplace.

4

Build a Great TEAM!

When you first started out in your business, chances are it was just *you*. Pretty much everything that happened in that business depended on *you*. If you didn't do it, it didn't get done. And doing it all in the early days gave you a sense of satisfaction and accomplishment. For the most part, there's nothing wrong with this. The problem arises when you begin to believe that as the owner, you're the only person who can do everything – and do everything right.

WRONG!

You Can't do it All

For your business to experience healthy growth, you *cannot continue to do it all*. Those who try, face a rocky road ahead.

Let's revisit the business plan we discussed in the first chapter. As you put your plan together, you defined how you want your business to grow and develop.

Ask yourself, do you want to just be *self-employed,* or do you want to build your business as a valuable asset? If your goal is to create an asset that you will one day be able to sell, then you'll need to rely on other areas of expertise to accomplish that goal.

As a business owner, you might be a control freak, but you must *let go of total control.* You cannot find a successful company in the Fortune 500 that runs with the CEO alone. That CEO knows and understands the concept of putting together teams of skilled, competent people.

Think of TEAM this way:

Together

Everyone

Achieves

More

As John C. Maxwell says in his book title,

"Teamwork Makes the Dreamwork"

Other Areas of Expertise

The reason a CPA goes to college for four years to get a degree, then trains as an apprentice for two years, is that it takes hours and hours of education and skills training to be a good CPA. It's no different than the way you achieved your licensing. The work you do is a skill. Do you have the skills to be a CPA? If not, then you'll definitely need an accountant.

Having an accountant on your team may seem obvious, as does having a good insurance agent and a trusted banker. But have you considered having a marketing expert on your team?

This person has studied marketing, works in it, is skilled in it, and constantly operates in that environment. He or she lives in that world. If you're not skilled or knowledgeable in this area, you may need to hire someone to support and help you grow this facet of your business.

You cannot do it all. What are your best contributions to your business? You need to know what your strengths and weaknesses are.

I Can't Afford It

If you think you can't afford to hire experts to assist you, ask yourself this: can you afford *not* to call in the experts? If you know your vision and your goals, then you're going to understand the tactics, the resources, and the budget needed to help get you there.

Do a cost analysis. Let's say you need a bookkeeper, but only part-time, which would typically mean about 20 hours a week. But when it comes down to actual productivity, it might require about 10 hours a week. That hardly seems like a wise expenditure.

So why not hire a virtual bookkeeper based on the actual productivity instead of hiring someone to come into the office several days a week? Now you've added to your team, you've called in an expert, and you're not wasting money paying for hours that are not being used.

Virtual Team Members

We live in a more collaborative economy than ever before.

We also live in a world where technology has brought things into existence that were unheard of only a decade or so ago.

You can find experts – affordable experts – by outsourcing on the Internet. This way you are leveraging a wide variety of mindsets, which could end up making you a lot of money. You have to:

- Know the experts are out there.
- Know how to find them.
- Know how to utilize them.

Two of the most popular outsourcing websites are www.Elance.com and www.Guru.com.

Using these sites you can find such experts as bookkeepers, virtual assistants, website builders, marketers, SEO experts, and so on. The list is endless of the talent that's available.

To use these resources, you create a job post and the *providers* bid on that project. You then are free to choose which provider, if any, you want to use. You set the price you want to pay. Each provider has a profile showing his/her past work and feedback from other clients. You are never working blind.

Beginning to outsource to grow your business often means stepping out of your comfort zone. A business coach can help you sort through the noise, do the research, and qualify the resource. Again, it's another great use of a team member.

Essential Team Member

Here's another example of team building. Because of the *Lone Ranger* mentality, many contractors make an attempt to save money by using voice mail, or worse yet, an answering service, to take phone calls. Ever hear the cliché, *You never get a second chance to make a first impression*? Never is that saying truer than when someone calls your business.

That potential customer is calling because they have a problem – it's a problem that they hope you can solve. But then they hear something like:

"Thank you for calling XYZ Contractors. Please leave your name and number and I'll get back with you. I return calls between three and four each afternoon."

This first impression tells the caller you can't handle the call in a personal way, and s/he may feel put off. It also gives the impression that your company isn't big enough to manage the problem.

I have no heat. My roof is leaking. The wind knocked out a window.

The problem is serious to the caller, and it should be serious to you. Serious enough for you to have a well-trained, customer-service person on the other end ready to take the call, to answer questions, to assure them that your workers can solve the problem, and then to schedule the technician to come out. The same well-trained, customer-service person will also do the follow-up calls making sure the customer is happy with the completed work.

Cutting corners by using voice mail or an answering service is a poor way to grow a business.

Selfishness

Another thing about attempting to do everything yourself, is that it becomes selfish, and selfishness is not an admirable trait. It's certainly not the trait of a leader. But that is often the mindset. It goes like this:

Why should I pay someone else to do it when I'm sure I can do it? Then I'll have more money for myself.

It's time to leave your ego at the door – egotism and selfishness are definitely first cousins, and neither one will help build a successful business.

When you're in the field working with an apprentice, it's easy to slip into the pattern of not fully training that person because you're sure you can do it better. But replicating yourself creates value. When something is teachable, valuable, and repeatable, that's value. It's scalable.

Scalability simply means the business can handle a growing amount of work in a capable manner. It's the ability to grow and accommodate that growth. For instance, when you have half a dozen well-trained technicians in the field, then your company is more than able to handle extra customers efficiently and effectively.

Any business that is not scalable is not salable.

This all goes back to your business plan. If you're thinking about ultimately selling the business, a buyer would prefer to see a team of highly trained technicians who are able to handle projects without the owner looking over their shoulders all day.

Summary

Where are you when it comes to building a strong team? Are you satisfied with just an accountant, an insurance rep, and your voice mail? Are you satisfied to feed your ego by telling yourself you can do it all?

Or are you ready to take things up a notch and become the business that people love to call because they know you'll give them personalized attention.

Are you the business that stands above the competition because an expert marketer has helped you design a logo and is teaching you how to build your personal brand?

Are you the business that caters to quality customers because you have a business coach who taught you how to court them?

It's up to you.

Chapter 4 Action Steps

- If you've been guilty of trying to do everything yourself, stop and take stock.
- Rank your current team members from one to five, with one being the weakest.

- Check out the outsourcing sites such as www.Elance.com and www.Guru.com to see what's available.
- Check out the possibility of using a business coach to help train you in team building.

5

Create Training Systems

Training. What does that word mean to you, and how does it factor in to your business? Make an honest assessment, and see if there might be some fine-tuning needed in your company in this area.

Here's what I see in most contractor businesses.

- Technicians are usually trained in the field and on the job. (Some owners find even this basic training difficult because it's easier and quicker to do it themselves.)
- Bookkeepers are typically trained for their positions.

And that's the extent of training in most contractor firms.

This limited view and understanding of the importance of training cripples the business. It leaves so much undone and compromises the levels of potential success.

Training All Employees

In the companies that I coach and work closely with, I encourage the training of *all* employees. Here are just a few of the benefits. Quality training:

- Improves employee performance.
- Shows employees the performance level they are expected to achieve.
- Gives them the basic skills to carry out their tasks.
- Gives them an understanding of the company and the industry.
- Builds their confidence.

- Reduces *call backs* in the business.
- Increases customer satisfaction.

Not only do well-trained employees perform better, they often come up with ideas of how to improve processes, which, in turn, boosts company growth. And if they see a fellow employee not performing correctly, they step up and show how it should be done. As a result, each employee feels like s/he is adding value to the company. (People naturally *feel* better when they perform better.)

On Board with Your Vision

Structured training and development programs ensure that your employees have the skills and knowledge to achieve your vision. They are fully aware of what your expectations are. Regular training in key functional areas informs everyone. Such training might include anything from safety to administrative tasks.

Of course, this is only doable and workable when you *have* a vision, and you *have* a system for carrying out that vision. An integral part of carrying out the vision is to have a *teachable* and *repeatable* training system in place. Such a training system is worth a lot of money to your company

Not every job or task can be repeatable, but 80 percent of field service work can be trained via a system. This develops your quality control system and identifies individual needs for training. You'll know who is doing well at which task and who needs extra training before being released to work solo. Who needs such training? Every employee in the company in every department--sales, marketing, bookkeeping, operations, etc.

Every employee needs to be trained in best practices and told how their skills contribute to the bottom line of the business. An investment in training systems and partners are critical to the company's wealth-building process. The return is a sustainable, repeatable process you can employ with anyone in the company, no matter who they are, no matter what they do.

Common Objections

If employee training is so crucial, why is it neglected in so many contractor businesses? Here are the most common objections I hear:

- Lack of time
- Lack of knowledge of how to implement training

- Ignorance of how to find training resources
- Lack of the right people to carry out training
- Uncertainty as to the benefits of training

Training is not a task that you as the owner must take on yourself. It can be contracted out, by either a marketing firm or perhaps a business coach. Remember, you don't need to do everything. What you need is a good team to make it all happen.

Call in the Experts

Product manufacturers and supply houses are excellent training resources. They have a vested interested in the correct installation and use of their products. Use such resources to your advantage.

The same is true for software manufacturers. Say you've purchased a bookkeeping or a scheduling system. Many such companies have trainers who come in-house. Once you have one or two employees who are adept at using the system, they can train others.

I encourage business owners to require office staff to sit in on product training. It's good for them to know what is being serviced and see it from a customer's perspective. This also gives them an understanding of what they're selling and what they're billing.

Another frequently overlooked training area is in customer service and customer relations. Your staff must know how to answer the phone, how to bring a customer on board, how to do customer follow up, etc. Such training never happens by accident. You must approach it purposefully and with specific intent.

Don't overlook other professionals in your business as possible trainers. This might include your accountant, your attorney, your insurance agent, and your business partners. Such individuals have a world of knowledge, and their input is invaluable.

Grasp the Importance

It all starts with you, the owner, the one in charge. Until you fully grasp the importance of employee training, nothing will happen. You're the one who must see how this step will enhance your business, cause profit margin to grow, raise employee morale, and create a happier workplace.

It all comes back to the plan. Does employee training fit with your vision?

Anything that is scalable, or builds value in a business, is teachable and repeatable. And if it's teachable and repeatable, there should be a training set up to tech it.

Include Training in the Work Schedule

Consider setting in place a systematic training of all employees on a regular basis. Let's say you schedule training for the first two hours of the last Friday of the month. Attendance is mandatory, and every employee knows it.

Once you make it a priority, you'll start to see positive changes in your business. You'll see it begin to chug along, exactly as it's designed to do.

Summary

This is your business; this is your brainchild. Nothing will happen until you set it in motion. And you'll never set something in motion that you don't consider a priority.

This is why it's imperative that you research the difference employee training makes in the overall success of a business. Once you grasp the importance, you'll be more willing to implement it.

If employee training is lacking in your business, you are cheating yourself, your business, your employees, and your customers. Is it worth it to ignore something so important?

Only you can decide.

Chapter 5 Action Steps

- Take stock of your own business operations, and honestly assess where training ranks in your priority list.
- Educate yourself on available training and discuss employee training with business partners or a business coach.
- Ask key employees for their input regarding employee training.
- Schedule training time at least once a month for all employees

6

The Yellow Pages are Dead

Now for a few tough questions:

Do you have the sales skills needed to sell your products and services?

- Do you have current marketing skills and knowledge?
- Can you effectively market what you're trying to accomplish with your business?
- Is there a difference between sales and marketing?

Fingers Walk Away from the Yellow Pages

There was a time when all a contractor needed to know about sales and marketing was how to create the most effective Yellow Pages ad. Back then, people used that thick book religiously to locate and hire local contractors.

The Yellow Pages advertising salespeople, of whom I was one for many years, pointed out that the most effective ads had the following features:

- Large size for high visibility.
- Color in the ad.
- Phone number in big, bold print.
- Appearance in several YP books (some were designed for suburbs and local areas).

Today phone books and Yellow Pages go in the recycling bin. Your customers have moved into a digital universe. And if you don't move with them, you'll be left behind.

Sales versus Marketing

Most contractors confuse the terms *sales* and *marketing,* supposing them to mean the same thing. They do not. By the end of this chapter, you will not only understand the difference, but you'll be better equipped to use both to propel your business to greater success.

Part I – Sales

Whether you realize it or not, you are always selling. You're always making some kind of impression with customers, potential customers, business partners, employees, and even your community. The idea is to be more focused and more purposeful about what and how you sell.

Not everyone is a gifted salesperson. Selling well requires empathy, good listening skills, and reacting without over-reacting to emotional objections. Selling is the art of bringing what the customer needs on their terms.

What Customers Look For

Do you know what your customers are looking for in a contractor? If you did, you could design your business to communicate that you do indeed meet those needs.

This is not a mystery. There are online sites designed to tell the general public exactly what they *should* look for in a contractor. Some lists are quite extensive. Here's a brief list you can add to as you do more extensive research. The public is looking for:

- A reliable referral from direct experience of family or friends.
- Licensing with no filed complaints or disciplinary action.
- Insurance (ask to see certificates) – Workman's Compensation and General Liability.
- Longevity: in business more than ten years with the same name.
- A physical business office and address.
- Positive current references from at least five customers.
- Specialization in the work.

Such customer priorities should become your selling points. Train your customer service reps to use them in sales presentations and with potential customers.

While not everyone is a born salesperson, there are some basic skills anyone can learn in this area.

Your company needs a consistently full pipeline, or you'll struggle to meet your sales goals. (You do have sales goals, right? These should be part of the plan you put together in Chapter 1.)

Prospecting

Unfortunately, very few companies teach sales people how to prospect effectively. Most simply rely on prospecting methods such as cold calling or networking, but there are so many other options:

- Asking for referrals.
- Approaching customers who haven't purchased from you recently.
- Speaking at industry conferences.
- Writing articles and blogs.
- Joining associations and actively participating.
- Looking for additional opportunities to sell deeper to existing customers.
- Arranging weekly coffee, breakfast or lunch meetings.

The key is to dedicate a significant amount of your weekly schedule to prospecting activities, regardless of how long you've been in business.

Questioning

Although this sounds like a fundamental concept, most of the salespeople I've met in the last fifteen years fail to effectively execute the practice of questioning. When they do ask questions, they ask low-value questions that do little to engage their prospects:

- "Are you the decision maker?"
- "What's your budget?"
- "What do you know about our company?"
- "Are you interested in saving money?"
- "What are your needs?"

Asking high-value questions is much more effective. These are questions that encourage the prospect to share information about his or her needs. High-value sales questions can transition into tough, penetrating questions. For example, if you were a kitchen remodeler, you might consider asking:

- "What does your dream kitchen look like?"
- "What challenges did you have in the old kitchen that you would like to resolve in a new kitchen?"
- "What impact is that having on your ability to entertain?"

- "How much time would you like to save when making meals?"

- "How important is this project compared to all the other projects you could do to improve your home?"

- "What could potentially prevent this from moving forward?"

- "What internal challenges do you need to deal with before this project gets the go-ahead?"

When you develop the ability to ask high-value questions, you'll stand out from your competition, while also learning more about your prospect's specific situation.

Listening

You can ask the best questions, but if you don't listen to the answers, you're losing valuable sales opportunities. Active listening means really hearing what people say. It means asking clarifying questions when the other person says something vague or that requires elaboration.

True listening means that you stop multi-tasking during a telephone conversation. Focus your full attention on that person.

Listen for underlying meanings, clues and cues, and respond accordingly.

One of the most effective ways to show a prospect that you've listened to and heard what they have said is to quickly recap the major points they mentioned as being important to them.

Presentation Skills

How are your presentations? Consider these two vital components:

- Content. Many salespeople include too much information in their presentations. Resist the temptation to tell everything. Only discuss the aspects of your offering that are critical for your prospect to know. And always open by discussing the buyer's situation – not your company's.

- Form. The more important a potential sale is for you, the more critical it is to rehearse that verbal presentation. Improve your skills by videotaping the presentation and then watch it, paying close attention to your pace, timing and delivery. Watch your body language, gestures, and facial expressions. It can be painful to watch yourself in action, but, believe me, it's highly effective. Watch yourself, then work on polishing that presentation.

Rapport Building

In spite of today's technology, developing a personal connection is still important in the sales environment. People still buy from people. Creating rapport with someone means connecting with him or her. You should be able to speak your prospect's language and to demonstrate that you understand the problem s/he faces.

For example, if a client has a leaky roof and it's been patched several times, and you know that the best solution is to replace the roof section, or the complete roof, be empathetic. Help the client understand that you've seen others who continue to patch their roofs and in the long run spend more money than if they had replaced the roof in the first place.

When you execute this properly, you not only develop rapport, you also position yourself as an expert.

You can also establish rapport by outlining the goal of your sales call, confirming the time that's been allotted and then finishing early. No one will EVER complain about a sales meeting finishing early!

Objection Handling

Objections are a natural part of the sales process. It's how you respond to them that can make or break a deal.

What are the objections you hear most frequently? Write them out. Now determine the most appropriate rebuttal. As you practice, remember these three key points:

1. **Empathize.** This means verbally stating that you understand, respect or appreciate the other person's concern. "Mr. Smith, I understand that you have some budget concerns."
2. **Clarify.** Restate the objection back to the prospect in your own words to ensure that you clearly understand it "So you see the value in this product, it's just that the purchase exceeds the budget you had allotted, correct?"
3. **Seek Permission.** Ask the person for permission to offer a solution. "Mr. Smith, May I discuss a few options?"

Follow this process and most people will be much more receptive to hearing your solution.

Persistence

To achieve long-term success in sales, you *must* be persistent. Just keep in mind there's a difference between being persistent and stalking someone. Persistence means finding creative ways to keep your name in your prospect's mind. If the potential customer is evaluating bids, schedule consistent calls with them to understand where they are in the bid process. Answer any questions and address any issues that arise. Providing a pricing quote is not the end of the sales process.

Persistence means not allowing the first few no's to prevent you from pursuing high-value, legitimate sales opportunities. Persistence means asking for the business or the appointment, or posing the right questions, even if the prospect is going in a different direction.

Focus

Lastly, in sales, you need focus. A multitude of distractions will threaten to change your focus. Email, telephone calls, text messages, problems, and paperwork are just a few. Keeping your focus on the big picture, as well as the smaller details, can make the difference between success and failure.

This also applies to each sales call and meeting. Determine the key objective for each call and focus on achieving that objective.

It requires tremendous effort and energy to sell in today's hectic and competitive business world. However, you can improve your results and achieve a higher return on your investment by developing and applying these essential sales skills.

Are you hiring the most highly skilled people as your sales team? Are you doing all the sales calls? Consider the sales strategies and skills of your team, and your business' sales goals to keep your sales pipeline full and growing. Don't leave this vital part of your business to chance.

As you review this list of vital selling skills, it should clarify your understanding of selling.

Part II – Marketing

Marketing is what you do in your business to make selling easier.

Let's take a look at how marketing works and how it can elevate you far above your competition.

Marketing is the way in which you present your company, your products, and your services to the general public. Marketing is the activity of promoting and positioning yourself in your community and in the marketplace to your target customers. Marketing sets up your salespeople to be successful. Marketing consists of:

- Branding
- Products
- Delivery mechanisms
- Promotional strategies

Of these four, the most important is branding. Branding is what separates you from your competition. Why are you different? Why would someone contact you instead of your competitor? If you don't have a distinction, then you are competing on price alone. Brand sets the baseline for all your advertising and promotion strategies.

Branding identifies the value component of your business. It also allows you to target a certain type of customer. You'll remember when we talked about your *target market* in Chapter 1. I encouraged you to identify whom you wanted as your main customers. Once you identify those customers, you can market to that demographic.

Let's say your target market includes:

- Baby boomers
- Higher end income
- Families with dual income
- Families with children
- Commuters

When you know your customers, you know what they like; you know their neighborhoods; you know their habits; you know their wants and needs. Once you have that down, you can focus on your marketing and promotion.

Marketing is one of your key external communication strategies. Creating your image and building your brand sends a message to your potential customers. A big part of how you communicate is through promotion. This might include press releases, blogs, websites, and newsletters. It could be your logo, your mission statement, your business slogan or your community involvement. These promotions inform people outside your company who you are and what's going on in your company.

Logo

Your logo is one of the best ways to communicate to public who you are and what you do. A professional logo:

- Creates an image
- Says you are a real company
- Gives credibility
- Shows you are serious about your business
- Says you care enough to invest the time to design a logo
- Makes your customers feel comfortable in doing business with you
- Makes you look bigger than you are

All big successful companies have a logo. If you want your business to grow, you should have one as well. You can use it on everything: business cards, invoices, website, uniforms, trucks. It's the symbol for your company.

People want to do business with someone who is successful. Your logo is publically visible and conveys a lot of messages:

- Success
- Stability
- Longevity
- Good character

If you think obtaining a professional logo is expensive, think again. Many online services can create a logo for you inexpensively.

Community Involvement

The owner of the company for which I worked those first fifteen years of my career was ahead of his time when it came to marketing. For years he sponsored little league teams where his company name, logo, and slogan was emblazoned on the back of the jersey of every team member.

He became well known among the kids, their parents, their friends, and extended family members. Some of those team members later became his employees in the business. How's that for great promotion?

Eventually, his business became such a community mainstay

that other businesses on our street would use in their advertising our store as a landmark. That kind of advertising cannot be bought at any price.

What role can you play in your community that would cause your name and your brand to stand out? Brainstorm and come up with some ideas. Here are a few to get your started:

- Sponsor a sports team
- Support a local charity
- Host community meetings
- Creat scholarships
- Become a local expert

Freebies

Always be on the lookout for items that you can give away for free with no strings attached. In the old days, it was a soap dish or a calendar with the company name on it. Today it might be a download offered on your website for a free report or a how-to. Here are a few quick ideas for topics:

- "Attic Fans for Whole Home Cooling"
- "Improving Home Ventilation"

- "Radiant Floor Heating: Is It Worth It?"
- "Electric Heating Options for Your Shop or Garage"
- "The Importance of Air Duct and Vent Cleaning"

Make free reports like these available on your website, to establish you as an expert and give your site a more professional look, as well as creating good feelings about your company.

Learn from the Big Boys

Look at how stores like Lowe's and Home Depot draw people into their stores. Have you ever noticed their Saturday morning how-to workshops? How can you do what they do, but do it even better? Don't let them beat you. Learn how to make things special for customers and potential customers.

Website

Do you have a website? And if so, is it being maintained? Is it being used to its best potential?

The Internet is the new Yellow Pages. Your website is today's version of a Yellow Pages ad from the *old days*. Only your website is:

- Cheaper than a YP ad.
- Easier to edit, change, and adjust on the fly (it can be changed every day, if necessary).
- Interactive (No one could leave a comment or message on a YP ad).
- Portraying a professional corporate image.

Statistics show that small businesses with a website have a higher income than those who don't. Your website not only puts you into today's technology, but it is your greatest source of new customers.

Make the site easy to navigate and easy for visitors to leave comments and feedback. This is how *word-of-mouth* works on the Internet. This is also how you keep your followers informed. For instance, if you're sponsoring a local marathon raising money for a charity, you can splash that news all over your website.

Building a website is not expensive. You can easily find a capable, reliable website builder on sites such as www.Elance.com and www.Guru.com. (Remember we mentioned this kind of outsourcing in Chapter 4.)

Some contractors mistakenly believe that they will get lost on the gargantuan World Wide Web, when in fact, it's the opposite. You will actually be much more likely to be *found* when you have a website. You should understand the concept of keywords in your website and consult with your web developer about the best strategy to allow your company to rise to the top of search engine results. Some small businesses use their town name in their URL. You don't need to beat out all the contractors in the country, or even your state. But you do want to try to get to the top of the list for contractors in your vicinity. Believe it or not, it really doesn't take that much marketing to get there.

Be visible where people are looking, and that is *not* in the Yellow Pages. The new catch phrase is, "Just Google it." You must be visible to the people who seek you. Your website is your workhorse--one that never sleeps.

Summary

You should now be clear on the distinction between selling and marketing. Each area demands your attention and input.

Whether you are the salesperson or have salespeople on your staff, you need to know the most effective sales techniques -- what works and what doesn't.

You can't sell if you have no prospects, and marketing will pull in the prospects.

I strongly advise having outside consultants come in to train your staff in both sales and marketing. Once you bolster this facet of your business, you will see strong, healthy growth in your company.

Chapter 6 Action Steps

- Learn the difference between sales and marketing.
- Develop a sales strategy; develop a marketing strategy.
- Invest the time to brush up on your selling skills. (Consider bringing in a trainer.)
- Assess the strengths and weaknesses of your current marketing strategies.
- If you don't have a website, acquire one immediately.
- If you have a website, use it to its maximum effect.
- If you don't have a professional logo, acquire one immediately.

- Brainstorm ways to be more involved in community events.

7

Automated Systems Improve Your Bottom Line

Service contractors have struggled for years and lost money due to poor job scheduling, illegible invoices, lack of invoicing for products and hours, poor customer communication, and time sheet accuracy of their technicians. Field Service Management software offers a solution to these problems.

Field Service Management is a software solution that offers

these benefits for your company:

- It gives a contractor ability to find business info without digging through paperwork.
    - You can keep all your client information together, from contacts and locations to important documents and even job history.
    - You can see where current customers are coming from and which jobs are driving the most revenue.
- You can capture and keep track of client phone calls and important documents.
- Job scheduling is automated and optimized based on geocoding of customer addresses. The system is a paperless environment where technician receive job assignments and complete invoices on a tablet or laptop in the field. Inventory items and pricing are controlled in your backend systems, eliminating pricing and parts description errors.
- Dispatching becomes paperless for the office staff and the technician. There is no need to call the technician to

notify him/her of last-minute customer changes. Email and text messaging provides a quick and efficient way to communicate with the field.

- Time sheets are built into the systems and collect on job times and idle times accurately.
- Reports are available to manage customers, job summaries, time sheets, and products and service sales.
- Field service management integrates with accounting software so billing is real time and accurate when the work is completed.
- More efficient job assignments reduce fuel costs.
- Some systems integrate asset tracking into the software so you can track trucks and equipment.

Many software providers offer a cloud based solution offering service contractors a managed software system with monthly fees. This is a pay-as-you-go approach and does not need IT skills on site.

The evolution of mobile technology has made these solutions affordable and practical for service contractors. Everything from

Smartphones to tablets are affordable and durable for field technicians to use on their jobs. The use of mobile technology will save your company time and money and allow a focus on key areas in sales and marketing to grow your business.

The article below is a reprint from David Crary, Hindsite Solution. It offers a great summary of the current technology and how it can change a contractor's business.

"5 Technologies Radically Transforming the Field Service Business"

By David Crary

Posted on Wed, Jul 23, 2014

Mobile technology and cloud based services can change the way you do business. Using mobile technology will not only save you time and money, but it will allow you and your employees more time to invest in sales, marketing and customer service. Business owners are continuously looking for new technology solutions. Consider the five tools listed below to help you drive your Field Service Business forward.

1. Smartphones

Smartphones can help your Field Service Business by:

- Easily downloading and uploading important business files
- Giving employees easy access to the entire client base

- Automatically updating customer information to multiple devices
- Giving immediate access to important documents and apps that can be read or edited in the office or on the road
- Offering GPS navigation and mapping apps to assist with service calls
- Offering synchronizing options to save time
- Offering mobile banking and accounting options
- Showing job details available in the field in real-time
- Showing customer history information
- Keeping accurate statistics when services are delivered by employees

2. Tablets

Storing data in the cloud and using tablets is another great option for your Field Service Business. Tablets can help your Field Service Business by:

- Allowing invoices to be sent directly from the job site
- Offering the ability to use a cloud based electronic calendar
- Helping employees manage appointments from anywhere
- Offering employees the ability to read and edit documents directly from the tablet
- Offering synchronizing options to save you time managing customer information
- Providing a long battery life for doing business
- Offering a light and portable device for employees to use on the go
- Offering employees a way to share videos, websites and presentations with fellow colleagues, business partners and customers

3. Payment Processing

Mobile payments and banking are becoming more and more popular with consumers and small business owners. Now you can send invoices, make estimates, manage sales and expenses with mobile technology. It's all about convenience for customers and reducing your costs. Mobile payment processes can help your Field Service Business by:

- Offering credit and debit card payments to your customers by using a mobile device
- Creating invoices and doing estimates for customers with ease
- Offering assistance to your employees managing sales and expenses
- Making it convenient for customers to pay for services by phone, tablet or laptop
- Distributing coupons through the payment process for repeat business
- Creating loyalty perks for those customers who have an on-going business relationship with your company

4. Field Service Software

As a small business owner, you're always looking for ways to improve your business processes and get rid of paper forms. Field Service Software [see http://hindsitesoftware.com] can help you operate your business more efficiently and help you automate time consuming processes [again, see website]. It's a powerful solution to helping you manage your entire field service operations. Field Service Software can help you by:

- Improving the efficiencies of your field processes
- Increasing productivity of your field workers by saving time
- Offering customers and employees real-time reporting options
- Providing easy schedule management for your employees
- Managing service calls with ease
- Managing equipment costs, invoicing and dispatching

- Improving customer communication
- Helping generate and manage new customer leads
- Handling repair records and parts ordering

5. Mobile Printers

You have a mobile work force, why not provide a mobile printer for you field service employees? It may be time to give your employees a portable office on the road. It will help them save time, money and increase productivity. This portable option will give them freedom to make calls, deliver services, offer contracts and deliver receipts. Below are some benefits of using mobile printing for your small field service business.

- Mobile printers can be connected with Bluetooth to GPS units for your business vehicles
- Easy and convenient mobile printing for invoices, receipts, contracts and important documents
- On-demand printing from anywhere your employees may be working
- An easy way for employees to edit and revise documents on the go
- Allows printing from multiple devices
- Mobile printers are durable and can withstand being carted from place to place
- Mobile printers are easy to operate, portable and self-powered

Technologies are evolving fast, some of which can drastically improve your business. If you haven't tried out some of these options, start doing some research and see if one or more of these technologies can boost your field service business.

The Hindsite Solution offers service contractor businesses a centralized system to manage their everyday business. It is a total field and business management tool encompassing Contact Management, Scheduling, Routing, Field Data Management, Billing, and Reporting. David Crary, founder of Hindsite Solution, developed the software package based on his own irrigation business needs. "

Summary

So many systems and programs are available, yet few service-contracting businesses take the time to incorporate them and use them to grow their businesses. In this chapter, I've only skimmed the surface of what's available and how you can integrate them into your business and reap the benefits they offer.

By not availing yourself of these amazing tools, you are leaving a LOT of money on the table. Why continue to cheat yourself, your family, and your employees? Learn more about the available automated systems and how they can specifically benefit your business.

Technology is your friend. By automating your business' operational processes, you'll make them more efficient and cost effective.

Chapter 7 Action Steps

- Conduct a cost assessment to determine where you spend the most money.

- Check out what automated systems are available for those areas.

- Ask your employees for their input about automated systems.

- Revisit your original business plan and determine how automated systems will help fulfill your vision and goals for the company.

8

Accountability

I'm not accountable to anyone. I'm the boss."

Although usually unspoken, this attitude is common among many contracting business owners. Yet accountability is a key factor in business success.

Large, successful corporations have a board of directors and a team of business advisors all working together to keep those in charge accountable. Many corporate leaders have personal business coaches who also act as accountability partners.

Stand by Your Word

Accountability, in its most basic form, is simply doing what you say you're going to do. It's standing by your word. This shows those around you that you have integrity, and it's reflected in your actions.

We tend not to think about accountability. Yet running the business doesn't mean you shouldn't evaluate your accountability and be accountable to someone or even to several people.

No One to Challenge You

It's a heady thing to be in total control of an operation such as your own business. The problem is, there's no one to challenge you if you don't get your tasks completed. Or if you start bending your own rules. Or if you slough off your business goals. Under your own supervision, it's easy to make excuses, to get distracted, to tell yourself, "It wasn't really that important."

Being accountable to yourself doesn't work. You need a

partner who will be straightforward and honest with you.

Selecting an Accountability Partner

After you formulate your business plan, as outlined in Chapter 1, you need to articulate it to someone you trust and respect. It will be that person to whom you are accountable for your own follow-through.

In your business, it might be a manager, bookkeeper, CPA, supervisor, or business partner. It might be another small business owner in a non-competitive field. It becomes even more effective when two accountability partners are accountable to each other. You might also consider bringing a business coach on the scene.

Showing that you're accountable, you as the leader set the tone for your team. Your demonstration of accountability becomes the essence of your business structure.

Leadership Quality

Accountability is a crucial leadership quality, and being a good leader is critical to your success. In this way, you're leading by example. You're communicating your values and your vision.

Again, you must step back and look at the big picture. What are you trying to achieve? Do you want a job? Do you want to be self-employed? Or do you want to build a viable business that one day will be a strong asset that is salable? If it's the latter, then you need to make accountability an integral part of your business model.

Summary

The idea of accountability, and having a specific accountability partner, is often overlooked in the hectic day-to-day demands of running a business. This doesn't make it any less important. If you find yourself saying one thing and doing another, especially if this has become prevalent in the way you run your business, it's time to take stock. How will your goals, dreams, and visions ever come to pass?

The most difficult part of working with an accountability partner is taking the first step. After that, you'll wonder how you ever got along without this key person in your life.

The next chapter illustrates not only why you need an accountability partner, but why you should articulate your company vision and goals to another person, on a regular basis.

Chapter 8 Action Steps

- Stop trying to be accountable only to yourself.
- Make a list of possible accountability partners (are people you know and trust).
- Present the idea to two or three of these people.
- Meet with at least two of these individuals on a regular basis.

9

Freedom in Your Future

As a skilled contractor, you probably started your business because you knew, and were licensed to perform, a particular skill. During the "building" phase of your business, you secured customers and projects, hired employees, bought equipment and trucks, invested in advertising, and other key activities.

That brings you to the point where you are right now.

Important Questions

Here are a few pointed questions:

- Could you sell your business today?
- Do you want to have a retirement income?
- What would happen if you were injured and could no longer work in the business?
- Are you ever able to leave your business for a few days and take your family on a vacation?
- Do you have a succession or transition plan?

Your business is your blood, sweat, and tears and is probably your most valuable asset. But did you ever consider whether it has a value, or a return on investment?

Not the Answer

In my experience, once a contracting firm owner decides to become less involved, whether it's voluntarily or due to illness or injury, s/he usually downsizes to manage the business, or just closes the doors.

But closing the doors is the not the answer! If you've built a customer base, hired employees, bought products and provided services, your business has intrinsic value to your community.

My goal is to teach you the key drivers of how to build value to grow, and then one day be able to sell your business, so that it brings value to you and others. I want to show you what makes your company a valuable asset, so you know where to focus your time and efforts to maximize your hard work.

Think about the value of your company from the potential buyers' view. Let's discuss some of the key factors buyers consider and how and why these are essential for you to create value.

Is the Company Dependent on You?

First, a company that is totally dependent on you, the owner, is vulnerable. Communicating your vision and goals, along with documenting your business processes, policy and procedures, is how you begin to allow the business to be less dependent on you. I have seen contractors who made all the decisions: buying, hiring, marketing, sales, and dealing with customers. Everything had to go through that one individual for approval. This dependency puts the company at risk if something ever happens to the owner. How does your business measure up in this area?

Diversification

This also points to why building a team is so important. Dependence on a few customers, a few employees, or a few suppliers creates the same problem as when the company is too dependent on you. Diversification of these key groups means a higher probability of company success if anything should disconnect a few key groups. Strength comes from having many good customers, employees, and suppliers. You don't want all of your revenues tied to a few customers, your key management assigned to a few key employees, or your key products tied to a single supplier.

Ability to Manage Cash

Financial performance and growth potential is critical. Previously, we discussed the Key Performance Indicators. Your company's ability to manage cash is high on any buyer's list. Your company needs to have consistent and predictable sales and quickly collectable accounts receivables. You need to pay your suppliers on time and receive a good return in your assets.

A successful company is predicated on the present value of your future cash flows. The profitability and future revenues are collective to your company to build new customers, build new markets, build new products, or to potentially cross-sell your products and services into other areas. The marketing strategy of your company needs to consider the *now*; but in order to create value, your company brand needs to withstand the test of time.

Create a Unique Brand

Standing apart from your competition equals value. If all contractors offer pretty much the same products and services, your company's value lies in building your particular, distinctive brand in the markets you serve. You must differentiate your company so it stands out amongst the masses.

Beyond logos and slogans, there are plenty of ways to create a unique brand. Most contractors offer basic labor and products as their only offerings. But there can be so much more. For example, if you are in the HVAC business, consider getting into the outdoor or specialty grill business. Bundle those services to complement each other, from both a service and a sales perspective.

Watch the trends in your industry and position yourself as technologically advanced in the new computer-driven controls in appliances and home products. Think outside the box; make your company an innovative and quality leader in your industry. Market those key messages to your current and potential customers. Differentiation makes you less dependent on a market price and instead be judged by the value you offer.

Take Care of your Customers

And finally, customer satisfaction is your homerun! Customer management and relations are the most important investments you can make and the most rewarding.

Here's one recommendation that could change your business and increase your sales. Make a follow-up call on every service call you make. Then send a thank you note with an invitation to visit your company showroom or website for a free gift! *It will make your customers want to invite you over for dinner.* These are the kinds of relationships that build value in your business.

Your company should have a written policy on customer service practices that covers time limits to return phone calls, to respond to emergencies, and to respond to disputes. Review these processes often with all of your employees to make sure everyone knows and follows them.

Conduct customer surveys at least twice a year, and preferably, quarterly. Survey questions should elicit usable information that shows you where you are excelling, so you can boost those areas, as well as where you need improvement, so you can address those issues.

Measure and quantify customer satisfaction as key valuable data of your company. Your customer satisfaction score then becomes part of your value statement to a buyer, to a lender, and to outside customers. Being able to prove customer satisfaction is a key asset of your business.

Summary

There you have it – the foundational practices you should, without fail, factor into your business to build value. It's up to you to get things moving. Much of what I recommend is not difficult to do;

it's a matter of awareness. It's taking the time from your already-overloaded schedule to think about your future and that of your company.

Building value is much more than simply *running a business.* It's time to change direction, and start building a salable business that will serve you and your family for years to come.

Action Steps

- Go to www.wisebusinessadvisors.com and take the Sellability Score Quiz.
- Set up a review of your 27-page Sellability Score Report with **Lynn Wise.**
- Schedule a Discovery Session with **Wise Business Advisors** and build an action plan to increase your contracting business financial performance and create a path to build true value in your business.
- Create a Freedom Plan and stick to it. *Don't wait!*

Conclusion

I began this book by telling you about my background and my inside connection with the world of service contractors. I also explained how my career mission is to reach out and help other service contractors to maximize their businesses. There is no reason to struggle along, barely making it, running from job to job, but never making progress, as with that hamster wheel I mentioned in Chapter 3.

You deserve better than that. So does your family. So do your employees. I've pointed out a number of mistakes that I see service contractors making repeatedly.

Conclusion

So much more is possible. I hope this book has expanded your view, brightened your outlook and enlightened your understanding.

Grasping a concept is one thing, but putting it into action is another. Resolve now to take at least one action step (from the ends of the chapters) each day, to forever alter your course.

I stand ready to step in and provide the assistance, encouragement, and insight to guide you along this journey. Please don't hesitate to contact me. (See my contact info in the **About the Author** section.)

Thank you for coming on this journey with me. I encourage you to keep this book at your fingertips as a ready reference and guidebook whenever you need it.

And remember – I'm in your corner…

Lynn Wise

About the Author

Lynn Wise entered the contracting business at age eighteen as a dispatcher for a local plumbing and HVAC repair and remodeling company. Over fifteen years, she learned how to operate and manage a successful contracting firm, helped increase sales, and eventually became an equity owner in the company.

She left the firm to earn her MBA in finance, then spent more than nineteen years in corporate sales and management.

Her entrepreneurial spirit finally took center stage, and she went on to use her practical and formal education to create, own and operate five successful small businesses in the areas of retail, distribution, and direct sales.

As a struggling entrepreneur starting out, Lynn would have loved to have had a step-by-step guide by someone who had been through it and achieved success. Now, having become that person herself, Lynn so closely identifies with the small-business owner/contractor that she wants to use her extensive knowledge to help others achieve greater success and turn a business into a salable asset.

Lynn wrote *Build it! Grow it! Sell it! Nine Steps to a Thriving Contracting Business* to help contracting company owners develop the management and executive skills to grow their businesses. Most contractors know that money is made in the field, and that's what leads many of them to go into business in the first place. While some do survive in business, the sad fact is, many more fail because they're too busy to manage the financial and strategic direction of their companies. They never learned to *THRIVE*!

Lynn knows what it means for a contracting business to die a slow, painful death. But she also knows what it takes for such a business to thrive. It's all here in her book, *Build it! Grow it! Sell it! Nine Strategies to Build a Valuable Contracting Business.*

Contact information:

Lynn Wise

   Website: www.wisebusinessadvisors.com

   Email: lynn@wiseba.com

   Phone: 772.834.8513

www.ingramcontent.com/pod-product-compliance
Lightning Source LLC
Chambersburg PA
CBHW072036190526
45165CB00017B/953